Published by:
Plum Street Press 1507 7th Street, #625,
Santa Monica, CA 90401

SHIFT

---

64 Ways to Raise Your Vibration and
Contribute to the Healing of the Planet

By...
Sally Walsh

SHIFT

Table of Contents

Introduction...

Yesterday I was clever
     So I wanted to change the world
Today I am wise
     So I am changing myself

              ...Rumi

"The only shift that can awaken and renew us is the one that comes from the transformation of our inner substance."

~ Baron Baptiste

SHIFT

How to Use This Book...

The 64 Ways in Shift are designed to be used in an
ascending order. Each of the eight sections are in an
order that makes them easy to follow and the
sections themselves are in a progressive order. If
you are enthusiastic and motivated you could also
do well working on more than one section at a time.
For example, while you are reading Wayne Dyer's
first book, Your Erroneous Zones, you might also be
working on your body and/or your thinking. Start
slowly, and add as your consciousness expands and
you are able to handle more.

Enjoy each new place and then move on as you feel
the inner urging or outer discomfort prodding you
to make a change. Remember that as you heal, you
raise your own vibration, which contributes to the
healing of those around you. There is no need to
have a judgment of yourself or others about what you
or they "should" be doing. Give yourself permission
to be enough. You are enough right where you are
even as you challenge yourself to do more.

This book isn't designed to be read in a week and
passed along. It's designed to be a road map for your
spiritual future. It's meant to be a companion - a
friend, even - on your spiritual journey. It might be
something you keep forever.

It's NOT the answer. It leads you to the answers you
are seeking. It's a tool. A blueprint.

Section One: Educate Yourself

ONE: Read a Book or
Watch a Video by Wayne Dyer

I recommend reading Wayne Dyer's books in chrono-logical order whenever possible, starting with Your Erroneous Zones. I read it when it first came out in the 1970's and it gave me the courage to leave a toxic marriage.

I continued to read Wayne Dyer's books when he wrote new ones over the years as his growth often seemed to parallel mine or be a little ahead. Whenever I came to a stagnant or stuck place in my life I would say, "It's time for Wayne Dyer to write a new book." And sure enough he would! I remember when Your Sacred Self came out. I cried when I started reading it because it was so what I needed.

The reason reading the books in order can be helpful is that you are constantly building on new insights as you progress at a manageable rate. Doing too much too soon or starting ahead of where you are can overwhelm and derail your progress. If you find you are studying what you already know just move through it faster. A little review never hurt anyone!

It's interesting how I read Wayne's books in the 70s and then had the chance to meet him with my grandson and daughter in the 90s and then last year my daughter ran into him and connected with him on the streets of NYC. He feels like a personal part of our lives.

Section One: Educate Yourself
TWO: Mindvalley Academy

Mindvalley offers free online presentations and meditation downloads and classes you can buy. It is an unending resource for spiritual materials and inspiration.

http://mindvalleyacademy.com

SHIFT

Section One: Educate Yourself
THREE: Loving What Is by Byron Katie

Byron Katie's work is heart-centered. She uses four questions and a thing called a turnaround to help us see "problems" from a different perspective. She calls it The Work which is the underlying basis for all of her books. It is a tool which is both simple and effective. Katie's writing style is easy to follow and also entertaining and fun to read. From her website: www.thework.com Byron Katie leads you into a way of identifying and questioning the thoughts that cause anger, fear, depression, addiction, and violence. Experience the happiness of undoing those thoughts through The Work, and allow your mind to return to its true, awakened, peaceful, creative nature.

For free tools to do The Work, visit:
www.thework.com

Section One: Educate Yourself
FOUR: Read Power Versus Force
by Dr. David Hawkins

Whenever I have participated in an exercise or visualization about what I want most in life the first answer that pops up is always "enlightenment".

My understanding of enlightenment is that it has two parts: Self realization and God realization. I have used many tools for self realization over the years but until I read Power Versus Force I didn't really understand what progress looks like. David Hawkins' Map of Consciousness, which is reproduced in all of his books, delineates vibrational levels. The higher the consciousness level a person has the more they counteract those vibrating at lower levels, which is why, as you grow, you are contributing to the healing of the rest of mankind.

If you find this book slow going just read a few pages at a time while you work on something else. When Power Versus Force makes sense to you venture into some of Dr. Hawkins' later works.

Section One: Educate Yourself
FIVE: Read a Translation of the Tao Te Ching

The Tao Te Ching is an ancient treatise written by the legendary Lao-Tzu. Tao Te Ching means Book of the Way. It contains 81 short chapters or verses of wisdom for living. There are numerous translations and commentaries on the Tao Te Ching.

Wayne Dyer has written his commentary on the 81 verses in Change Your Thoughts Change Your Life. The acknowledgments page at the end lists ten versions of the Tao Wayne Dyer used while writing his book.

Stephen Mitchell's English translation of the Tao Te Ching is one of my favorites. Chapter 79 says, "...the Master fulfills her own obligations and corrects her own mistakes. She does what she needs to do and demands nothing of others."

A Thousand Names for Joy by Byron Katie and Stephen Mitchell is Katie's response to Mitchell's translation of the Tao. Katie's down to earth simplicity beautifully complements this ancient wisdom.

Two translations not mentioned by Wayne Dyer are by Ralph Allan Dale and Ray Grigg. Dale's beautiful book has two parts. The first includes the original Chinese characters, Dale's translation, and beautiful photographs. The second part is a repeat of the translation next to Dale's commentary which shows us how the Tao is still relevant to present day living

Ray Grigg's book, The Tao of Being, is written as what he calls a workbook. Each verse also includes an exquisite Chinese brush painting by William Gaetz. My favorite translation of any Tao verse by any author is Grigg's verse 22. "Soften to know. Bend to understand. Empty to fill."

The Tao is a book to read a little at a time as you absorb the wisdom. It is also something to return to when you are looking for inspiration.

Section One: Educate Yourself
SIX: The Four Agreements
by Don Miguel Ruiz

Don Miguel's agreements are beliefs or rules to live by. His underlying premise is that we all have agreements or personal rules which affect how we live our lives. The key is to recognize them and be aware of what we are choosing. His four agreements are suggestions that can help us live a better life. Don Miguel says if we live even one of these agreements consistently it will change our life.

The introduction is long. It may seem obscure, but it is powerful and insightful. Don't let it discourage you from getting to the agreements. They are simpler to understand - if challenging to implement.

Section One: Educate Yourself
SEVEN: Vasistha's Yoga

Vasistha's Yoga is an ancient scripture that was orally transmitted by temple monks for centuries before it was written down in Sanskrit. It is the teaching of the sage Vasistha as told to Lord Rama. He uses metaphors and entertaining stories that teach that all is Consciousness. Some things are repeated in the scripture including the following verse:

"This world appearance is a confusion: even as the blueness of the sky is an optical illusion. I think it is better not to let the mind dwell on it, but to ignore it."

What great advice from an ancient sage! Reading the chapters in order and in small pieces is helpful in taking it all in. Then you can go back and reread favorite parts for years to come.

Section One: Educate Yourself
EIGHT: Read On
As you go deeper you will be led to other sources of inspiration.

Dr. Michael Bernard Beckwith, the leader of the Agape International Spiritual Center in Los Angeles, has several powerful works to assist you. He can also be heard live or on the recorded services when you visit the Agape International Spiritual Center website at www. agapelive.com. Dr. Beckwith's books include Spiritual Liberation and Life Visioning, (a book that helps you align with your life's purpose in a deep and profound way) and he was a contributor to the movie and book The Secret.

Ernest Holmes has written several inspiring and life changing books. Creative Mind, his first book, written in 1918, is a metaphysical classic. It is one I return to again and again for reminders of Truth. Holmes says, "If the Truth is All, it must be everywhere." He also tells us, "We cannot attract to ourselves that which we are not." Creative Mind reminds us that we all have a creative mind and are only limited by our thoughts.

Neville wrote ten beautiful and inspiring books which can also be life changing. Two of the most well known are Awakened Imagination and The Power of Awareness. In Awakened Imagination Neville tells us, "What we imagine, that we are." If you decide to read Neville's works be prepared to have many of your old beliefs shaken up and more of your dreams come true.

Christian Larson is the author of The Pathway of Roses which was written in 1913. He tells us, "To serve the human race in the largest and highest sense, we must bring forth into living expression the truest, the best and the greatest that we can possibly find in the depths of our own sublime being." Reading The Pathway of Roses is like walking in a beautiful garden where we find inspiration about life's deepest mysteries. Christian Larson shows us how we can bring forth our best self and when we forget we can read his book again and again. Christian Larson wrote several other books, including the amazing Perfect Health, written in 1910.

Joel Goldsmith, like Neville and Christian Larson, was a great mystic and spiritual teacher. His inspiring books include A Parenthesis In Eternity, Living Between Two Worlds, and Living The Infinite Way. If you are ready to go deeper into your journey Joel Goldsmith can help you get there.

Section Two: Change Your Thoughts

ONE: Change Your Perceptions

Max Planck says, "When you change the way you look at things, the things you look at change." Many of the materials recommended in Shift help you to do that. See especially Creative Mind by Ernest Holmes and Loving What Is by Byron Katie.

Section Two: Change Your Thoughts
TWO: Practice Gratitude

"If the only prayer you ever said was 'thank you'
that would be enough."

~Meister Eckhardt

Thank you is such a powerful word whether spoken as a prayer or as a communication with another person. If we are not thankful for what we have what could possibly be the point of having more?

Attitudes of Gratitude by M.J. Ryan is a good place to start if you are gratitude challenged. Keeping a gratitude journal or starting and ending your day by saying what you are thankful for helps keep it flowing. Some days I think of one thing I am grateful for every hour on the hour. This can create a change of attitude whether you want it or not!

Section Two: Change Your Thoughts
THREE: Stalk Your Thoughts

"Those who do not observe the movement of their own
mind must of necessity be unhappy."

~ Marcus Aurelius
(Ancient Roman Emperor)

When you are feeling unhappy or dissatisfied
with a situation, a person, or life in general examine
your mind and ask, "What am I telling myself about
this?" If you are feeling unhappy or upset you know you
are telling yourself something negative.

Step back and observe your thoughts as though
you are an impartial bystander. What are you thinking?
Is it useful or edifying? Do you have something better to
think about? Are your thoughts uplifting someone? Try
focusing on what you want - not what you don't want.

Byron Katie's work is great for helping us examine our thoughts. She says. "I love my thoughts but I
don't believe them."

Section Two: Change Your Thoughts
FOUR: Affirmations

Affirmations are positive thoughts which help us to affirm the real truth. Replacing negative and depressing thoughts with positive affirmations helps keep us on track and out of the dark places. Personalize affirmations to fit your personality and circumstances. Great affirmations create happiness and self confidence.

Sign up for Hay House Daily affirmations to inspire you. Books by Louise Hay also contain great affirmations. When you can't come up with a good affirmation for yourself ask a friend to help you. It is sometimes easier to see the best for others than for ourselves.

Some people feel like they are lying when they say positive affirmations, especially about themselves. But those positive affirmations are actually the real truth and the negative judgements are the lies.

Section Two: Change Your Thoughts
FIVE: Complaint Free

The more we complain the more there is to complain about. We become a magnet for negativity and annoyances. I like to ask the question, "How bad is it?" Usually it's not very bad and we are blowing it out of proportion. Even if things seem really bad it is important to shift the energy and contribute to healing or resolving something rather than magnifying it.

The Complaint Free World by Will Bowen is a great guide to creating a complaint free life. I also love the concept of distinguishing between complaining and stating a fact. I have had some hilarious discussions with family and friends about 'stating facts' when everyone knows we are actually complaining!

www.acomplaintfreeworld.org

Section Two: Change Your Thoughts
SIX: I Am

Always say (or think) something positive after the words "I Am".

"I Am" is who we are. If you say, ""I am stupid," your self will believe it and you will create that in your life. If, however, you say, " I am an intelligent person who made an error," you leave room for correcting the error and creating the life of an intelligent person.

Section Two: Change Your Thoughts
SEVEN: The Subconscious Mind

What are your beliefs and rules and where did they come from? Are you happy with them or do they keep you stuck? The Four Agreements and other works by Don Miguel Ruiz can help us examine the often subconscious rules we live by. He calls the filling of our young minds the domestication of the planet. Many of our underlying beliefs became part of us when we were very young and unable to discern truth and wisdom. We were taught other people's rules and beliefs and without realizing it we made them our own. Now is the time to examine what serves you and what is sabotaging your happiness and success. Now you can choose from a new place of understanding and bring the subconscious into the conscious.

Examples of (untrue) belief systems we carry around: I am unlovable, unworthy, unsafe, invisible, etc. Remember, you created them so you can discreate them.

Section Two: Change Your Thoughts
EIGHT: Getting in the Flow

When you have learned to calm your mind so it is not constantly running away with you it will then be possible to start tuning into your intuition. When we have a relaxed and calm mind it is easier to give up our resistance to what is and move into the flow. This is the place where life becomes more relaxed and peaceful. We make decisions more easily and live with less stress. We move into the space of being able to hear the still small voice of wisdom and love which directs us into the flow of ease and grace.

Shakti Gawain's Living in the Light teaches us about becoming a channel for the creative power of the universe. This is our purpose. All of the materials recommended in Shift will help you to align with your true Self and tap into intuition and wisdom.

SHIFT

Section Three: Heal Your Body

ONE: Massage

Massage is good for body, mind and soul.
Getting a massage is a great way to embrace self-care.
Releasing emotional patterns and tension from the
muscles and fascia will lead to improved physical and
emotional health and personal well-being. Massages
are relaxing, a great way to pamper yourself and can
contribute to your overall quality of life.

SHIFT

Section Three: Heal Your Body
TWO: Martial Arts, Tai Chi, Yoga, and Qigong

When you practice these mind/body disciplines you prepare your body and mind for the discipline to sit in meditation. These practices, in themselves, are also healing for the mind and body. They help create energy, balance, flexibility, peace of mind, self confidence, and overall well being. These classes and gatherings are also a great place to meet like-minded people.

Section Three: Heal Your Body
THREE: Essential Oils

Our sense of smell can have a strong impact on our moods, clarity of mind and energy levels. Essential oils can boost our immune systems and aid in detoxifying the body. Orange and ginger are uplifting while lavender is calming. Frankincense is wonderful for meditation. Oils, scented candles, soaps and bath oils are a few of the ways to pamper yourself with aromatherapy. My personal favorite oil is doTerra.

Section Three: Heal Your Body
FOUR: Movement

The key of course to adding any type of exercise into your life is to find at least one thing you'll actually do. Find something that works for you. Keep it simple. When you keep it simple, or make it something you like, and not just a chore, it becomes as important as brushing your teeth or combing your hair and you will do it. If you resist exercise maybe you can change your mind about it by making it something fun. Try making it something you do with a friend. Why not make exercise part of your social life? Some people do fine with brisk walks and light yoga while others have bodies that do best with very intense workouts. Just doing something regularly is the key.

It is important to note that your blood type may have an effect on the type of exercise your body does best with. For example, according to Live Right for Your Blood Type, by Dr. James D'Adamo some of us don't lose weight or reach optimal wellness with strenuous activity. For example, people with blood type A are the ones most often better off with yoga, tai chi, pilates or walking and may become exhausted with strenuous activities, while an O type does well with vigorous activity. Type B is about balance: cardio, strength training, and some yoga. AB can combine type A and B activities. The research behind these theories can be found in Dr. D'Adamo's book.

Movement helps us heal. It offers many benefits, including improving sleep, increasing energy and dissipating stress. It can increase endorphins and lift depression to keep us mentally as well as physically fit. Daily activities such as gardening, shoveling snow, cleaning house, walking the dog, or climbing the subway stairs help keep us fit while also accomplishing something else at the same time! Whatever you do, get up and move. Haven't you heard? Sitting is the new smoking!

Section Three: Heal Your Body
FIVE: Seek the Underlying Factors in Health

Louise Hay's classic book You Can Heal Your Life is also available on video. Louise recounts her own story of illness and healing. She relates illness to underlying emotions and thought processes. For example, shoulder problems are about making life a burden. She offers affirmations for healing such as: "I choose to allow all my experiences to be joyful and loving." Knees can be about fear and willpower issues. Louise offers, "I bend and flow with ease, and all is well." You Can Heal Your Life has a chart with symptoms, probable causes, and suggested new thought patterns. It is a valuable resource you will find yourself returning to often.

Section Three: Heal Your Body
SIX: Donna Eden's Energy Work

Energy medicine helps to restore energies that have slipped out of balance. Donna Eden turned to energy medicine for herself when she was ill many years ago. She has since become a great teacher and inspiration to others. The Little Book of Energy Medicine is a great place to start. It has simple explanations and lots of pictures to help you learn how to balance your own energy.

Donna's other book, Energy Medicine, is much longer with more information and explanations. Browsing through the pages at a bookstore or library can be an eye opening experience that may entice you to learn more. Donna also has an online presence with short videos and she offers classes and trainings in different locations.

https://www.facebook.com/EdenEnergyMedicine/

Donna's website is: http://innersource.net/

Section Three: Heal Your Body
SEVEN: Supplements and Diet

What you eat and how you care for your body greatly affect your moods and energy levels physically, emotionally, and spiritually. Yogis and other deep meditators often eat vegetarian diets because eating lightly makes it easier to meditate. It is important when choosing your food to do what works for you. Educate yourself about nutrition and also use your intuition because your body knows what it needs.

Remember how important your whole life is when choosing foods. Joshua Rosenthal, Director of the Institute for Integrative Nutrition, teaches about a term he coined: "primary foods." "Primary foods are the things that nourish you outside of the food you eat. Consider your spiritual practice, an inspiring career, regular and enjoyable physical activity, honest and open relationships that feed your soul and your hunger for living as your primary foods." (Integrative Nutrition, Inc., Fundamentals 2) In other words, if you have a challenging relationship, a challenging boss, a job where you work too much, or some other stressor in your life you may be more prone to binge eating or poor food choices. Perhaps you don't need a diet change, but a new job. Doing things that make you happier will inspire you to eat better. Conversely, eating better can give you the boost you may need to change other areas of your life.

The gluten free "fad" that some people mock works miracles for others. "One person's food may be another person's poison," says Rosenthal. The gluten in our foods today is much harder to digest than what we ate in the past. The symptoms of gluten intolerance are many and include physical symptoms and mood imbalances. Many who try a gluten free diet for a short while feel so much better that they decide it is well worth the effort to stick with it.

Supplements can be a helpful way to give your body the nutrients it might be missing from the food you eat. Finding ones that are made from whole food sources and keeping it simple is the easiest way to get started. Supplementation means to add to. Start with the best diet you can eat and then add supplements for optimal wellness. Leading experts on superfoods and nutrition include: David Wolfe, http://www.davidwolfe.com/ and Bob Gilpatrick, www.boomerboost.com/health-videos; see this page for some techniques and more supplement information (full disclosure: Bob Gilpatrick is my brother).

Section Three: Heal Your Body
EIGHT: Your Body Listens to Your Mind

Be careful what you think and say about your body. It has ears to hear! If I think, "Wow, I'm so tired," my body succumbs to exhaustion. If, instead, I say, "It's time for some rest," my body has permission to relax. Just like I always want to say something positive after "I am" I also want to be positive when I talk or think about my body. Here is a sample affirmation for creating a more healthy body:

"I am happy and grateful that my body is abundantly healthy."

Section Four: Work Through Emotions

ONE: Breathe

Breathing deeply is calming and invigorating. When we are stressed we tend to breathe shallowly and rapidly. Sometimes people even hold their breath without being aware of it.

Suggested exercise:

Sit or lie in a relaxed position. Hold your hands over your abdomen. Inhale deeply and feel your abdomen expand. Exhale and imagine pushing your abdomen all the way back to your spine to expel all the air. You can also count how long you inhale and exhale. Inhaling and exhaling evenly creates balance and helps with depression.

Example: Inhale for a count of four and exhale for a count of four. Repeat as many times as you want.

Inhaling longer than you exhale helps with tiredness or sleepiness when you need to stay awake.

Example: Inhale for a count of six and exhale for a count of four.

Exhaling longer than the inhale helps with anxiety and panic attacks. People who are anxious tend to take short breaths without exhaling much. Exhaling completely helps to push out accumulated stale air and contribute to calmness.

Example: Inhale for a count of four and exhale for a count of six.

SHIFT SHIFT

SHIFT

Section Four: Work Through Emotions
TWO: Learn about Stress

Stress is not what happens to us. It is our reaction to what happens to us that creates the stress response in our body and mind. Something happens. We have a thought about what happened. The thought then leads to a calm or stressful reaction. Stalking your thoughts can be a great way to intervene in perceived stressful situations.

Donna Eden says emotional pain occurs because we are out of sync. I learned an exercise from her that helps me get back in sync. (My friend and I use the term "discombobulated" when we are out of sync.) Put one hand on your forehead to return blood to your forebrain. Now put your other hand on the back of your head to calm your fear point. This is a very simple exercise that can give amazing results.

SHIFT

SHIFT

Section Four: Work Through Emotions
THREE: Aromatherapy

Essential and organic oils can be very helpful in altering and lifting your mood and helping find balance. For example: Lavender is known to be relaxing, orange is calming, and spearmint is uplifting. Eucalyptus clears the mind (I find it also helps clear my sinuses). You can inhale from the bottle, put a drop on your skin, or use a diffuser. Using a diffuser with a favorite oil can be a wonderful aid in falling asleep. Bath oils and lotions provide great aromatherapy too. I like to blend coconut oil with one of my favorites to make a foot rubbing cream. Don't be afraid to pamper yourself and loved ones!

SHIFT

Section Four: Work Through Emotions
FOUR: Understand Anger

If you have worked on changing your thoughts you will likely notice that your anger issues have already lessened in intensity and duration. The emotion of anger comes from telling ourselves that something should be different than it is.

There is a saying that if your anger lasts longer than 5 minutes it is old anger. Your reaction to what seems to be causing your anger is colored by past experiences which are influencing your current situation. Ask yourself what your thoughts are telling you that is contributing to an angry reaction. Anger can lift you out of lower energy levels. Sometimes you may need to visit the anger place to get out of victimhood but it is not a place to stay. Let anger tell you it is time for change while moving on to a place of peace. Long term anger is not good for your health, either emotionally or physically. Remember: Resentment is like taking poison and waiting for the other person to die.

There are many classes, books and other materials to help you understand anger. The Power of Now by Eckhart Tolle and Loving What Is by Byron Katie help get to the root of anger when we incorporate their teachings. Materials by Gerald Jampolsky, which are based on attitudinal healing, http://www.ahinternational.org/podcasts/downloads and the second of Don Miguel Ruiz's Four Agreements (Don't take anything personally) help in seeing things differently. When we see things differently our reactions can change and we are in control of our own emotions.

Section Four: Work Through Emotions
Five: Forgiveness

Forgiveness is for the person doing the forgiving, not the person being forgiven. When we need to forgive someone it is because we have somehow judged or found someone guilty. We forgive by recognizing that judging is not our job. There is a difference between judging and noticing. We may notice that someone is doing or saying something which may cause harm and take steps to prevent or heal it. But holding angry or vengeful thoughts mostly hurts us and does nothing to contribute to healing solutions.

Wayne Dyer says, "Forgiveness is the most powerful thing you can do for yourself on the spiritual path. If you can't learn to forgive, you can forget about getting to higher levels of awareness." Any place you have unforgiveness is a place where you will be stuck. And while you are forgiving others remember to forgive yourself!

Suggested forgiveness tools:

Radical Forgiveness by Colin Tipping
21 Days to Forgive Everyone for Everything
By Iyanla Van Zandt
A Course in Miracles

Section Four: Work Through Emotions
SIX: Laughter

The old saying, "Laughter is the best medicine," has a lot of truth to it. Laughter is good for body and soul and for relationships too. Try laughing with someone for no reason. You'll soon find yourselves laughing for real. Have you noticed how when adults laugh babies will join in even though they don't know why we are laughing? Laughing is part of being human. Read the Sunday comics or a humorous book. Watch a funny movie. One of my favorite laughing memories is of watching Elf with my husband and grandson. My grandson and husband have infectious laughs which make me laugh even more.

SHIFT

Section Four: Work Through Emotions
SEVEN: EFT

EFT stands for Emotional Freedom Technique. Dr. George Goodheart, DC, Dr. Roger Callahan, Dr. John Diamond, MD, and Gary Craig all deserve credit for creating EFT. It has more commonly come to be known as tapping, because it involves tapping on acupuncture points. It has its roots in Chinese medicine, Thought Field Therapy, Neuro-linguistic programming and energy medicine. *It's so simple that anyone can do it!* Nick Ortner, author of The Tapping Solution, calls it acupuncture without needles. EFT can change or retrain your brain because it interrupts the stress cycle and fight or flight response. You can tap while focusing on a particular issue, emotion, or health challenge to change unwanted patterns. With some practice you can learn to do EFT yourself and create new patterns in your brain. This can result in newfound emotional freedom and joy in your life. Visit: http://www.thetappingsolution.com or https://vimeo.com/92533046 for more information.

Section Four: Work Through Emotions
EIGHT: Feelings Come From Thoughts

When you are experiencing negative feelings
ask yourself, "What am I telling myself?" What
are you saying out loud or inside your head that is
causing the emotional upset? Examine the thoughts
which are contributing to your reaction and give
yourself permission to change those thoughts. Byron
Katie's Loving What Is is a great tool for teaching us
how to examine our thoughts. When your thoughts
change your feelings will follow.

Section Five: Like-Minded People

ONE: Join a Yoga or Tai Chi Class

There are enough kinds and levels of yoga classes to suit a wide range of interests and abilities. Tai Chi is slow moving and focused. In addition to creating calmness it contributes to strength and balance. Many of these classes are mini social groups with students often getting together outside of class. They also tend to be welcoming to newcomers.

Section Five: Like-Minded People
TWO: Meet Up With Your Tribe

www.meetup.com is a way of connecting with people who live in your region and share similar interests. When you log in and create a free account you can use search terms like consciousness, spirituality and meditation to learn about groups that are meeting and when. You can even start your own group!

Section Five: Like-Minded People
THREE: Mindful Magazines

Find and read free publications like Body Mind Spirit
Guide and Natural Awakenings. These are national
publications with local editions. They can be found in
health food stores, libraries and spiritual centers. They
are packed full of information, interesting articles,
calendars of local events and contact information for
local practitioners and centers.

Body Mind Spirit Guide: www.bodymindspiritguide.com/
Natural Awakenings: www.naturalawakeningsmag.com/

Section Five: Like-Minded People
FOUR: Book Clubs

Think about starting a book club. While you are working on educating yourself invite others to join you and provide support and a way to discuss and process what you are reading. This will keep you motivated and committed and can also be fun. Remember not to take yourself so seriously that you forget to enjoy the process.

Section Five: Like-Minded People
FIVE: Give Yourself The Gift
of Attending a Live Event

As you begin to read books and magazines and do online research you will see retreats and lectures advertised. Don't be shy. Sign up for something with one of your favorite teachers or topics. It will open up a whole new world for you. You will meet amazing people who share your interests and your enthusiasm and you may even begin life long friendships. Some events offer scholarships or free attendance for volunteering. Keep your heart and mind open. Who knows? Someone may even offer you a free ticket!

Section Five: Like-Minded People
SIX: Facebook Groups

I know many people who have met new friends they originally connected with on FB. Facebook minimizes our degrees of separation. It's a playground for big people and can be an outlet or an inspiration for many topics and interests. When someone asks you to "like" something look carefully to see if you're interested in it so you will receive more of what you like.

Section Five: Like-Minded People
SEVEN: Make the Shift

The Shift Network: Accelerating the Next Evolution was founded by Stephen Dinan. From their website: The Shift Network empowers a growing global movement of people who are creating an evolutionary shift of consciousness that in turn leads to a more enlightened society, one built on principles of sustainability, peace, health, and prosperity.

www.theshiftnetwork.com

Sign up for the mailing list (called the free Catalyst e-zine) then check your email inbox to access the free information and online courses. After you sign up for the free mailing list and click register it takes you to a page where you can upgrade by paying. The free access will be in your email inbox.

Section Five: Like-Minded People
EIGHT: Spiritual Centers

Unity Churches, Agape International Spiritual Center, Marianne Williamson's Monday night meet ups, Centers for Conscious Living, and various retreat centers such as Mt. Madonna Center in Northern California, Joshua Tree Retreat Center in Southern California, and Omega Institute for Holistic Studies in New York, are all wonderful places to find like-minded people.

Section Six: A Course in Miracles

When we really desire to evolve (actually removing everything that is not You), people, events and epiphanies show up for us. As we wash away our ego aspects, the spiritual Self can shine through. A Course in Miracles is a tool many have used to tame their egos and get in touch with the spiritual Self. It has been highly recommended by David Hawkins as a way to raise your vibration. While the book itself may seem large and daunting it is designed to be digested in small bites. I did the daily lessons three years in a row, skipped a year, and then did them a fourth time. I still review from time to time and study parts of the texts, always surprised at new insights no matter how many times I read the same thing because each time I am coming from a new place.

Section Six: A Course in Miracles
ONE: Read May Cause Miracles
by Gabrielle Bermstein

If A Course In Miracles seems daunting try starting
with Gabrielle Bernstein's six week mini course.
Gabrielle is a student of the Course and so comes
from that perspective. She offers daily exercises
which can jumpstart your growth if you are ready to
commit to it. Her lessons are gentle and affirming
and are best done by following the plan she outlines
for morning and evening. A great way to begin and
end your days!

Section Six: A Course in Miracles
TWO: Do the Daily Lessons for Students

The Workbook for Students in A Course In Miracles has 365 lessons. My preference is to start on January 1 and do one lesson a day for the year. You can actually start any day you want. Just start! If it takes more than a year that's OK. Do keep going until the end. Don't think you have to understand each lesson before you can move on. You can spend two days on a lesson if it seems important to do so. And don't guilt yourself if you miss a day here and there. Keep track of what lesson you are on and do not be tempted to keep starting over or do more than one lesson in a day. Each day builds on the previous one and some lessons will be repeated. David Hawkins found that a critical turning point seems to happen around day 75. So persevere until you get there and then you won't want to stop. Remember not to take yourself too seriously. Some friends and I read the first lesson together and laughed and laughed as we teased about each other's belongings having no meaning.

Section Six: A Course in Miracles
THREE: Read Books Based on A Course in Miracles

Gerald Jampolsky has written several books based on the Course. His book, Teach Only Love, is about his seven principles of attitudinal healing. They are beautifully simple, yet life changing when we learn them.

Marianne Williamson's first book, Return to Love, is very inspiring. Read it before you start the Course or while doing the daily lessons. Visit: www.marianne.com. Check out the video page for some great talks and interviews Marianne has done.

Gary Renard has written a powerful and entertaining trilogy: The Disappearance of the Universe, Your Immortal Reality, and Love Has Forgotten No One. These are helpful to read before, during or after studying A Course In Miracles. They will definitely cause shifting so be ready! It also makes more sense if you read the books in the above order.

Section Six: A Course in Miracles
FOUR: Read the Section called, "Text"
in A Course in Miracles.

Read it in small increments. I like to read one
section at a time and sometimes reread a section
before going on to the next one. It is not something
to hurry through or finish. You can reread it forever
because each time you will be coming from a new
place. So if you don't understand something it is OK
to move on because it will come around again.

Section Six: A Course in Miracles
FIVE: Manual for Teachers

Read the Manual and know that we all can be teachers for God just as we can all be students. Like the text, it is divided into sections. Go slowly without rushing or having an agenda in mind.

Section Six: A Course in Miracles
SIX: Read Supplementary Materials

There are also CDs and videos about the Course which can help you understand and heal at deeper levels. Ken Wapnick is one of my favorite Course teachers. His materials can be found at: http://www.acim.org/. This site is run by the original publishers of A Course in Miracles.

Section Six: A Course in Miracles
SEVEN: Try A Course in Miracles Support Group or Class

See if it is helpful to you and if it is a good fit. Be aware that without good leadership or understanding of the Course some groups may degenerate into complaining and forget that the Course, when applied to your life, is a tool for healing and moving out of that ego space. There is now a Course in Miracles app that's free for iPad, iPhone or computer users. You can get the app by searching the app store with "A course in miracles" or from the following site: http://www. jenniferhadley.com. This is the global ACIM group I have been enjoying: http://love.livingacourseinmiracles.com. www.meetup.com offers some ACIM groups too.

SHIFT

Section Six: A Course in Miracles
EIGHT: Attend a Lecture or Workshop

The best teachers bring the Course to life for us and show us how to use it in our daily lives. The more you do the easier it will get and the more it will impact and permeate all aspects of your being and become as natural as breathing. Marianne Williamson offers Monday night lectures in Los Angeles and other cities. She also offers this lecture online.

Sign up here: http://marianne.com/livestream-mondays/

SHIFT

Section Seven: Stillness

I move and breathe and have my being within the heart of God.

Goals and desires related to relationships, money, health and lifestyle are merely physical details of the spiritual journey. They are not the journey but can help sustain our body/mind while living a human experience.

ONE: Time

"Meditating five minutes a day is like *thinking* about putting on deodorant. But it's a place to start!"

~Laura Mitchell

Meditating is not about doing anything. It's about letting go. Michael Beckwith always says that there is no such thing as a bad meditation. He reminds us that being a meditator is called having a meditation "practice." Even three seconds of feeling a deep connection means that you have tipped over into transcending your mind. Meditation isn't about controlling your mind. It's about transcending it.

As you begin to meditate or sit in the stillness, be patient with your busy mind. No judgements! As you become more comfortable you can increase the amount of time you sit in meditation and also the number of times per day. Many people meditate morning and evening. If you can add a session in the middle of the day you speed up your progress even more. If you are wakeful at night or in the early morning see this as a nudge to meditate or pray. If you have a hard time settling down start by reading something inspiring or listening to peaceful music. There is no such thing as, "I can't meditate." There is only "relax and try again." If your body rebels against sitting, yoga classes can increase your flexibility and relaxation abilities.

Section Seven: Stillness
TWO: Deepak/Oprah

Deepak Chopra and Oprah periodically offer a 21 day meditation series. These are beautiful and inspiring and can be a great tool to help you feel comfortable with meditation or just help you move into a new space. The original series is always free and is then offered for purchase if you want to be able to continue to use it. To find a free meditation, go to the resources page of www.choprameditation.com or after you have registered you may use the following direct link and click on the "stream a free meditation" link. The free one is there - keep looking. Use the resource page to find it. Once you register you'll receive information on the next 21 day journey with Oprah and Deepak.

SHIFT SHIFT
SHIFT
SHIFT SHIFT
SHIFT SHIFT

Section Seven: Stillness
THREE: Evolutionaries

Craig Hamilton, the founder of Integral Enlightenment, offers meditation downloads, CDs, retreats, and once a month online Sunday meditations. Every fourth Sunday is his live Meditation for Evolutionaries. Craig created the Academy for Evolutionaries, offering practical spiritual tools and training that work well in the modern world.

Craig's website is:
http://integralenlightenment.com/academy/

Section Seven: Stillness
FOUR: Zen Mind, Beginner's Mind
By Shunryu Suzuki

Read this book anytime. (Buy your own copy - you'll be glad you did.) Be sure to read the introductory parts so you will know why you don't always understand it. Don't be attached to "getting" what you read and don't give up if it seems too hard. Just read it from beginning to end, one chapter at a time. And then in a few months, or even a few years, read it again. As your understanding grows more of it will resonate with you. It is a book to be read many times over a lifetime and each time it will be new to you.

Section Seven: Stillness
FIVE: The Stillness

"Within you there is stillness and sanctuary to which
you can retreat at anytime and be yourself."

Hermann Hesse

Meditation is not about getting something or becoming
something. It is about remembering your true essence. In the
Stillness you can remember who you are.

Suggested exercise:

Light a candle. Play some soft meditative music with no
words. Sit in silence for ten minutes or longer. Have pen and paper
handy to write a letter to yourself that tells the highest truth about
you and your life.

Here is a letter I (Sally) wrote to myself:

Dear Sally,
You are surrounded by beauty and love. All is not as it
seems. There is much joy and a plentitude of blessings. There is
no need for fear or pain, only love and joy. The air around you is
soft and caressing, the sky a beautiful blue canopy with pillow soft
clouds. The rain is a blessing of abundance. The road is smooth and
filled with wondrous adventures. To laugh and to love are all you
have to do. There is no effort. Living is effortless and joy-filled. Your
perfect home and your perfect love are part of you. There is no fear.
Only love. You are as beautiful as the beauty that surrounds you.
Love radiates from you to all around you. It fills your heart, your
soul, your entire being. You float through life as though sitting on a
cloud.

Love,
Life

Section Seven: Stillness
SIX: The Presence; Laura wrote this Facebook Post

The Presence

How could the words of any human being ever hurt, harm or endanger us when we are all a drop of the Consciousness... God - the omnipresence, the omnipotent, omniscience of All?

The Presence, not words are the guiding light of our soul's unfolding. Words from one cannot take away anything - for we have already been given all.

Within each of us, God has placed the seeds of greatness, prosperity, abundance, grace, health and wellness, brilliance, happiness and JOY.

So the next time you hear words that you think made you feel less than - whether it's from your significant other, a parent, a child, the curse/diagnosis from a doctor of something incurable or any other type of ridiculousness, just say no thank you and look deep within your own heart and say I'm so grateful God. Thank you God for having already given me all that this other says that I am not. Thank you for letting me know I am blessed in each moment. Thank you for this knowingness that the spiritual fact is that I am healthy, whole and divinely placed here on this planet.

God, I know that everywhere I am - YOU are. If I AM, then YOU are. No matter the time, place, or emotion I find myself in - YOU are. The masks of my perception are why I label what someone else says as having the power to harm or hurt me. Simply it does not.

I know that God is not by my side - God is EVERYWHERE- within and outside of me - up, down, all around and knowing that - what small little problem or egoic reflex of someone else could ever separate me from that feeling? This feeling that has become a knowing that I am a child of God. God is here, there, everywhere, in every moment, every place and every breath, every perceived heartache and any struggle I find myself challenged by. I know that I can just turn my eyes inward and feel the presence. The Love shall wash over me as I release and Surrender to the love, truth, beauty and goodness that are emerging for me, from me and surrounding me as soon as I can let it be.

And So it Is.

Section Seven: Stillness
SEVEN: Meditative Music and
Guided Meditations

Silent Journey offers the Zen Spotlight Daily Inspirations for free. It also has meditation materials which can be purchased. Deepak Chopra has an online presence and meditation CDs. Mindvalley has Omvana as a phone app and it is also available directly from their website. Karl Moore offers a Zen 12 meditation series which helps you gradually increase your meditation level. Try Amazon and your local book store for something inspiring. Once you start looking you will find what you are seeking.

SHIFT

Section Seven: Stillness
EIGHT: Spend Time in Nature

Being in nature can be restorative to your soul. Open yourself to the beauty of peaceful surroundings. Enjoy sunrises, sunsets, stars, and the moon. Listen for your own still, small voice. It is there inside you waiting to be heard. Walk on a beach, hike in the mountains, enjoy your own yard, sit on a park bench, grow a plant in a pot. The opportunities are endless for connecting with the earth and yourself.

Earthing
Research has proven that being connected to the Earth is healing and minimizes the effects of stress. In fact, "Earthing is a fast-growing movement based upon the major discovery that connecting to the Earth's natural energy is foundational for vibrant health," from the Earthing.com website. More from the website: "Go barefoot outside for a half-hour and see what a difference it makes on your pain or stress level. Sit, stand, or walk on grass, sand, dirt, or concrete. These are all conductive surfaces from which your body can draw the Earth's energy." When you Earth, the earth's electrical field is transferred to the body.

For more information please visit:
http://www.earthing.com

SHIFT

Section Eight: Kriya Yoga

ONE: Read Autobiography of a Yogi

This book by Paramahansa Yogananda, tells the story of Yogananda, who brought Kriya Yoga to America. It's a fascinating read and will awaken your hunger to learn more. Sri Yukteswar, Yogananda's Guru, said that, "Kriya Yoga is an instrument through which human evolution can be quickened." Yogananda called Kriya Yoga a spiritual accelerator. Is it time for you to speed up your evolution?

SHIFT

Section Eight: Kriya Yoga
TWO: YouTube

Subscribe to the YouTube Channel of Hamsa Yoga Sangh and Himalayan Master Yogiraj Siddhanath and watch some videos.

www.youtube.com/hamsayogi

SHIFT

Section Eight: Kriya Yoga
THREE: Search for Siddanath

Visit the Siddhanath.org website and sign up to be on the email list. Check out: http://www.siddhanath.org/mediagallery/yogiraj-books and look for the books by Yogiraj Gurunath Siddhanath. Wings to Freedom is a great start and when you are ready Babaji: The Lightning Standing Still is a true treasure.

Section Eight: Kriya Yoga
FOUR: Find a Teacher

Find a nearby Kriya teacher and reach out to learn the Kriya. The Siddhanath website shows Kriya teachers with locations and contact information. http://www.siddhanath.org

Section Eight: Kriya Yoga
FIVE: Begin Your Personal Practice

Don't be afraid to ask questions when you are confused. Be sure to read and reread any materials provided to you. They will help answer many of your questions and remind you of what you learned from your teacher.

Section Eight: Kriya Yoga
SIX: Attend a Retreat or Workshop

Being in the presence of a master or Guru is amazing and inspiring. It is an opportunity and gift not to be missed. The Siddhanath website has a calendar of events available around the world.

Section Eight: Kriya Yoga
SEVEN: Stay Connected

Once you learn the Kriya and other practices such as the Surya and Earth Peace meditation continue to attend retreats and get-togethers. Practice with your teacher as often as possible and meet to meditate with others.

SHIFT SHIFT
SHIFT
SHIFT

Section Eight: Kriya Yoga

EIGHT: Be Consistent

Having a daily practice is key to making progress. When you miss for a day or more recommit to the self discipline required to become a true Yogi. You will not regret it and the benefits are infinite. What you are seeking is your True Self. It awaits you.

SHIFT

SHIFT   **SHIFT**
SHIFT SHIFT
SHIFT FT
SHIFT SHIFT

About the Author
Sally Walsh

Sally Walsh is a licensed professional counselor and a certified Kriya Yoga teacher. She is the author of Joyful Parenting: Tuning into Your Child. Sally has been a member of Renaissance Unity since 1998 and loves to attend the Agape International Spiritual Center when she is in the Los Angeles, California area. She lives in Michigan with her husband and her pet rocks. She is the mother of three amazing children and the grandmother of two extraordinary grandsons.

www.ingramcontent.com/pod-product-compliance
Lightning Source LLC
Chambersburg PA
CBHW040035110426
42741CB00031B/105